LEARN

French

WORDS

window
la fenêtre
(lah fuh-neh-truh)

bedroom
la chambre
(lah shohm-br)

bathroom
la salle de bains
(lah sahl duh bahn)

living room
la salle à manger
(lah sahl a mahn-zhay)

kitchen
la cuisine
(lah kwee-zeen)

BY M. J. YORK • ILLUSTRATED BY KATHLEEN PETELINSEK

Published by The Child's World®
1980 Lookout Drive • Mankato, MN 56003-1705
800-599-READ • www.childsworld.com

Acknowledgments
The Child's World®: Mary Berendes, Publishing Director
Translator: Aline Baehler, Senior Language Lecturer of French,
New York University
The Design Lab: Design
Red Line Editorial: Editorial direction
Amnet: Production

ISBN 9781626873742
LCCN 2014930645

Printed in the United States of America
Mankato, MN
July, 2014
PA02217

ABOUT THE AUTHOR

M. J. York is a children's author and editor living in Minnesota. She loves learning about different people and places.

ABOUT THE ILLUSTRATOR

Kathleen Petelinsek loves to draw and paint. She also loves to travel to exotic countries where people speak foreign languages. She lives in Minnesota with her husband, two daughters, two dogs, a fluffy cat, and three chickens.

CONTENTS

Introduction to French

French is the language spoken in France. French is the main language of more than 25 countries. Some people speak French in Canada, Haiti, Belgium, and Switzerland, too. They also speak French in the Democratic Republic of the Congo, Madagascar, and many other African countries. They speak French in Vietnam and Laos, too.

French is a Romance language. Romance languages grew out of Latin, the language spoken by the ancient Romans. Spanish, Italian, and Portuguese are Romance languages, too. Written French is more than 1,000 years old.

French uses the same alphabet as English. It adds four different kinds of accents to vowels. The accents change how the vowels are said. They are:

acute accent: ´

grave accent: `

circumflex: ^

umlaut: ¨

French also adds a mark called a cedilla (ˌ) to the letter c: ç. It is pronounced like s in seat.

Some other letters are said differently than in English:

h is never pronounced.

ll is sometimes pronounced like yuh.

r is said further back in the throat with the back of the tongue (to feel the position, try to say "Gus").

s at end of words is often not pronounced.

qu is pronounced like k in Kate

v is sometimes pronounced like v in vote but sometimes like vw together.

y is pronounced like ee in sheep.

p, **t** and **k** are said a bit differently in French. Try not to let an extra puff of air escape from your lips.

Try to rest your tongue just behind your teeth for **t**, **d**, **s**, **z**, **l**, and **n**.

My Home
Ma maison
(mah meh-zohn)

window
la fenêtre
(lah fuh-neh-truh)

lamp
la lampe
(lah lahmp)

bathroom
la salle de bains
(lah sahl duh bahn)

bedroom
la chambre
(lah shohm-br)

television
la télévision
(lah tay-lay-vee-zee-yohn)

kitchen
la cuisine
(lah kwee-zeen)

cat
le chat
(luh shah)

living room
la salle à manger
(lah sahl a mahn-zhay)

sofa
le canapé
(luh kah-nah-pay)

table
la table
(lah tah-bluh)

chair
la chaise
(lah shehz)

In the Morning
Le matin
(luh mah-tan)

dresser
la commode
(lah kaw-mawd)

clock
le réveille-matin
(luh ray-veh-yee-yuh-mah-tan)

teddy bear
l'ours en peluche
(loors ohn puh-loosh)

doll
la poupée
(lah poo-pay)

pillow
le cousin
(luh koo-zan)

bed
le lit
(luh lee)

blanket
la couverture
(lah koo-vehr-tyoor)

MORE USEFUL WORDS

I like science.
J'aime les sciences.
(zhehm lay see-ahnss.)

I like art.
J'aime l'art.
(zhehm lar.)

I like music.
J'aime la musique.
(zhehm lah myoo-zeek.)

I like reading.
J'aime la lecture.
(zhehm lah lehk-tyoor.)

Can I please go to the bathroom?
Est-ce que je peux aller aux toilettes?
(ehs kuh zhuh pouh ah-lay oh twah-leht?)

Please help me.
Aidez-moi s'il vous plait.
(eh-day-mwah seel voo pleh.)

My name is _____.
Je m'appelle _____.
(zhuh mah-pehl _____.)

student
l'élève
(lay-lehv)

pen
le stylo
(luh stee-loh)

homework
les devoirs
(lay duh-vwar)

At the Park
Au parc
(oh park)

sky
le ciel
(luh syeh-ehl)

Let's play!
Jouons!
(Zhoo-ohn!)

friend (masculine)
un ami
(uhn ah-mee)

friend (feminine)
une amie
(oon ah-mee-yuh)

soccer ball
un ballon
(uhn bah-lohn)

MORE USEFUL WORDS

game
un jeu
(uhn zhouh)

sports
les sports
(lay spawr)

bird
un oiseau
(uhn wah-zoh)

sun
le soleil
(luh saw-leh-yuh)

swing
les balançoires
(lah bah-lahn-swar)

cloud
un nuage
(uhn noo-azh)

playground
le terrain de jeu
(luh teh-rehn duh zhoo)

slide
le toboggan
(luh taw-baw-gahn)

water
l'eau
(loh)

pond
un étang
(uhn ay-tohn)

flower
une fleur
(oon flouhr)

duck
un canard →
(uhn kah-nahr)

13

airplane
un avion
(uhn ahv-yohn)

offices
des bureaux
(day byoo-roh)

building
un immeuble
(uhn ee-mouh-bl)

bus
un bus
(uhn boos)

MORE USEFUL WORDS

train
un train
(uhn trehn)

truck
un camion
(uhn kahm-yohn)

stop
stop!
(stawp!)

go
allez!
(ah-lay!)

My Birthday Party
Mon anniversaire
(mohn ah-nee-vehr-sehr)

grandmother
la grand-maman
(la grahn-mah-mohn)

grandfather
le grand-papa
(luh grohn-pah-pah)

I am six years old.
J'ai six ans.
(zhay sees ohn.)

sister
la sœur
(lah souhr)

brother
le frère
(luh frehr)

cake
un gâteau
(uhn gah-toh)

MORE USEFUL WORDS

zero **zéro** *(zay-roh)*	eleven **onze** *(ohnz)*
one **un** *(uhn)*	twelve **douze** *(dooz)*
two **deux** *(douh)*	thirteen **treize** *(trehz)*
three **trois** *(trwaah)*	fourteen **quatorze** *(kah-tawrz)*
four **quatre** *(kah-tr)*	fifteen **quinze** *(kanz)*
five **cinq** *(sank)*	sixteen **seize** *(sehz)*
six **six** *(sees)*	seventeen **dix-sept** *(dees-seht)*
seven **sept** *(seht)*	eighteen **dix-huit** *(dees-weet)*
eight **huit** *(weet)*	nineteen **dix-neuf** *(dees-noof)*
nine **neuf** *(nouhf)*	twenty **vingt** *(vahn)*
ten **dix** *(dees)*	

19

At Night
Le soir
(luh swahr)

MORE USEFUL WORDS

Today is Friday!
C'est vendredi!
(say vohn-druh-dee!)

Yesterday was Thursday.
Hier c'était jeudi.
(yehr say-tay zhouh-dee.)

Tomorrow is Saturday.
Demain c'est samedi.
(duh-mahn say sahm-dee.)

Good night!
Bonne nuit!
(bawn nwee!)

bathtub
la baignoire
(lah behn-war)

I am tired!
Je suis fatigué!
(zhuh swee fah-tee-gay!)

22

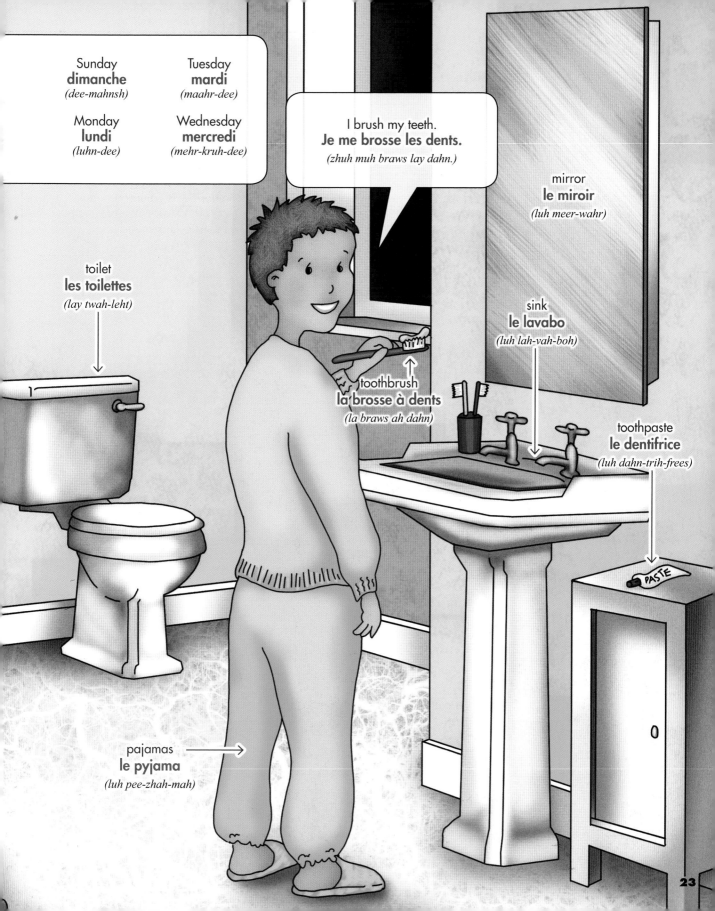

23

MORE USEFUL WORDS

Yes
oui
(wee)

No
non
(nohn)

ten
dix
(deez)

twenty
vingt
(vahn)

thirty
trente
(trohnt)

forty
quarante
(kah-rohnt)

fifty
cinquante
(sahn-kohnt)

sixty
soixante
(swah-sohnt)

seventy
soixante-dix
(swah-sohnt-dees)

eighty
quatre-vingts
(kah-truh-vahn)

ninety
quatre-vingt-dix
(kah-truh-vahn dees)

one hundred
cent
(sohn)

January
janvier
(zhohn-vyay)

February
février
(fay-vree-yay)

March
mars
(mars)

April
avril
(ah-vreel)

May
mai
(meh)

June
juin
(zhwee-ahn)

July
juillet
(zhwee-yeh)

August
août
(oot)

September
septembre
(sehp-tohn-br)

October
octobre
(awk-taw-br)

November
novembre
(naw-vohn-br)

December
décembre
(day-sohn-br)

winter
l'hiver
(lee-vehr)

spring
le printemps
(luh prahn-tohn)

summer
l'été
(lay-tay)

fall
l'automne
(loh-tawn)

good-bye!
Au revoir!
(oh ruh-vwar!)